The Lion Hunts
In The Land Of Kachoo

Written by Tina Scotford

Illustrated by Frans Groenewald

JACANA

A lion took a stroll in the light of the moon
Hunting Kachoo with his bowl and his spoon
He was on the prowl for an animal to eat
Something quite meaty for a midnight treat

He scanned the hills and the rocky terrain
Searching and hunting his royal domain

But everywhere the old lion went
He could not pick up even one animal's scent

The zebra, giraffe and brace of young buck
Were behind the bushes where they'd quietly snuck
Not moving an inch, nor making a sound
They kept out of sight in case they were found

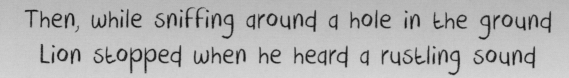

Then, while sniffing around a hole in the ground
Lion stopped when he heard a rustling sound

After scanning the area to make sure it was clear
He tapped the ground for the animal to hear

"Hello Mr Animal, and how do you do?
Please open your front door so I can come through"

The house belonged to a little mongoose
"He'll taste rather nice served with gravy and juice,"
Whispered the lion while licking his lips

When mongoose heard this, his heart did a flip!
Little mongoose burrowed deep into the ground
Faster he dug while not making a sound

"I said, open up! Or I'll growl and I'll roar! I'll use my sharp claw
To scratch down your door!"

The lion scratched, then roared and growled
"Where have you gone?" the lion howled

"Too late, Mr Lion, I've escaped through the back hole
Did I ruin your first course – juicy mongoose casserole?"

Away mongoose fled into the dark of the night
Leaving the lion to hunt by moonlight

Kachoo is long and deep and wide
On I'll go, the lion sighed
His throat was now scratchy and dry from thirst
But I need to find a cool drink first

While the lion drank from a pool of water
He spotted a hippo's very young daughter
She was standing on top of a gleaming brown mound
And her mom and her dad were nowhere around

"She's small but chunky, a fat young hippo
She'll taste rather nice with mashed up potato"

The lion purred while rubbing his tummy
When hippo heard this
she screamed out for mummy

He surveyed the area
looking about
Before greeting the hippo
and shouting out:

"Hello, young hippo
please sit over here
I've a secret to whisper
in your tiny ear"

The young hippo stood still while on top of the mound
Not saying a word nor making a sound
"I said, come on over! Or I'll growl and I'll roar!
I'll use my long claw to pull you ashore!"

And then the young hippo got taller and taller
The mound that she stood on rose up from the water
Who was that there? Where had she come from?
The mound that she stood on was the young hippo's mom!

The lion growled with all of his might
Then he flashed his claws
in the silver moonlight

"Too late, Mr Lion, she's with her father and I
Did we ruin your main course of mashed hippo pie?"

The mother and daughter swam under the water
And disappeared into the night

Again the lion was left alone to hunt
by the fading moonlight

The lion prowled the savannah grass
Still hunting for food
to break his long fast
Over the hills and over the plain
Searched the lion, again and again

His tummy now ached and loudly rumbled
"I need to eat," the lion mumbled

And then his luck appeared to change
When he spotted something rather strange

"What's that I see behind that log?
A snorting pig? A large warthog?"

"He'll taste rather good served with cranberry jelly,"
The lion said while patting his belly

I'll surprise the warthog
or bush pig I've seen
Thought the hungry lion
now feeling quite mean

Touch 'PAWS' engage!

Lion crouched down
and then snuck up to the log
Growling and roaring
he pounced on the warthog

But what did he see
when he sprung in the air?
Who was that waiting
with a deathly stare?
It wasn't the warthog
or a grunting bush pig
It was something more challenging
and very big!

The rhino was snorting and stomping his feet
"I'm not something that you should eat!"
The rhino warned before charging the lion

"You're right, Mr Rhino, there's no point in trying,"
The lion said, now avoiding the fray
Then he turned on his heel and scurried away

The lion skulked home in the dawn of the day
The hunt he'd planned had not gone his way
His head bowed down, his heart filled with sorrow
Perhaps I'll have better luck
under the moon of tomorrow

First published by Jacana Media (Pty) Ltd in 2012

10 Orange Street
Sunnyside
Auckland Park 2092
South Africa
(+27 11) 628-3200
www.jacana.co.za

In collaboration with 2sq Design (Pty) Ltd
© Text: Tina Scotford, 2012
© Illustrations: Frans Groenewald, 2012

ISBN 978-1-4314-0695-1

Editor: Dominique Herman
Designer: Jeannie Coetzee
Set in DK Crayon Crumble 22 pt
Job no. 001813
Printed by Tien Wah Press (Pte) Ltd

See a complete list of Jacana titles at www.jacana.co.za